CITIES OF THE WORLD

SYDNEY

BY R. CONRAD STEIN

CHILDREN'S PRESS®
A Division of Grolier Publishing
New York London Hong Kong Sydney
Danbury, Connecticut

CONSULTANTS

The Library of the Embassy of Australia, Washington, D.C.

Linda Cornwell
Learning Resource Consultant
Indiana Department of Education

Project Editor: Downing Publishing Services
Design Director: Karen Kohn & Associates, Ltd.
Photo Researcher: Jan Izzo

Visit Children's Press on the Internet at:
http://publishing.grolier.com

Library of Congress Cataloging-in-Publication Data
Stein, R. Conrad.
        Sydney / by R. Conrad Stein.
                p. cm. — (Cities of the world)
        Includes bibliographical references and index.
        Summary: Describes the history, culture, daily life, food, people, sports, and
points of interest in Australia's oldest, largest city and busiest seaport.
        ISBN 0-516-20593-5 (lib.bdg.)   0-516-26328-5 (pbk.)
        1. Sydney (N.S.W.)—Juvenile literature.   [1. Sydney (N.S.W.)]
I. Title.   II. Series: Cities of the world (New York, N.Y.)
DU178.S815   1998   97-29428
994.4´1—dc21   CIP
                                                    AC

TABLE OF CONTENTS

Most modern travelers fly to Sydney, Australia, aboard jet airplanes. But the best way to approach the city is by sea. Sydney is one of the world's great port cities. Every year, more than 4,000 giant cargo ships sail in and out of Sydney Harbor. The vessels carry millions of tons of goods. Countless small craft also ply the harbor. In the past, ships loaded with immigrants made the long voyage from England to Sydney. The immigrants sought a new life. They looked upon Sydney as the "Gateway to Australia." Many of the immigrants prospered in the new land. Australia enjoys one of the world's highest standards of living.

Ships steaming into Sydney Harbor today pass the city's striking Opera House. It is Sydney's most famous landmark. Completed in 1973, the great building has multiple shell-like roofs. The series of roofs is designed to represent the sails on a ship. The comparison to a ship seems appropriate. The building stands on Bennelong Point, which juts into the harbor. But Sydney residents are strong individuals. They are quick to voice their own opinions about the Opera House. Some claim it does not look like a ship at all. Instead it looks like a neatly folded dinner napkin. Others say it resembles freshly washed clothes fluttering on a line. This is Sydney, a place where all opinions must be heard.

Holding 3.5 million people, Sydney is Australia's largest city. It is not the country's capital.

That honor belongs to the city of Canberra. Experienced travelers claim that Sydney is one of the world's happiest cities. It is clean, prosperous, and relatively free of crime. A sunny climate allows residents to enjoy sports and the outdoor life. Only 200 years old, it is a young city by world standards. Perhaps youth is the key to Sydney's remarkable vitality.

This woman in a wildlife park is holding two baby Tasmanian devils, Australian animals that will grow up to be very vicious.

Above: A paperweight featuring the Sydney Opera House.

Opposite: A view of the Opera House

SIDERS

The people of Sydney are called Sydneysiders. No one knows the exact origin of the name. Some say the name comes from the fact that Sydney is north of the Murray–Darling river system, Australia's largest. Sydney is said to lie on the "Sydney side" of the Murray. Others maintain the name lies deep in the city's history. Sydney was once a British convict colony. Its inhabitants were condemned to live their lives far from home—on the "Sydney side" of the world.

Aborigines were the original Australians. Shown on this page are a young schoolgirl and a man with a boomerang.

THE CHANGING FACE OF SYDNEY

When World War II ended in 1945, Sydney's residents were over-whelmingly white and very, very British. Certainly nonwhite and non-British people lived in Sydney, too. Hundreds of dark-skinned Aborigines, the original Australians, resided in the city.

But crowds on the city's streets were generally a sea of white faces. Almost everyone spoke the English language. The vast majority of Sydneysiders had English, Irish, or Scottish backgrounds. That setting was quite a contrast to today. Now, the guitar-like strumming of *bouzouki* music drifts from Greek restaurants. In some districts, Italian or Vietnamese conversations are heard more frequently than English. Modern Sydney has its own Chinatown. Grocery stores in Chinatown sell exotic goods such as cuttlefish and a dried fruit called love prunes.

The astonishing changes in modern Sydney were brought about by the Australian government. After World War II, national leaders were eager to bring immigrants to the country. Authorities feared that Australia was under-populated and could not maintain its prosperity. Australia is as large as the United States. But in the late 1940s, the nation had only about 7.5 million people. This meant that all of Australia held only as many residents as New York City does today.

Children with Rainbow lorikeets at the Taronga Park Zoo

Above: An Australian boy

Right: Girls at Sydney Hospital rub the nose of this pig statue for luck.

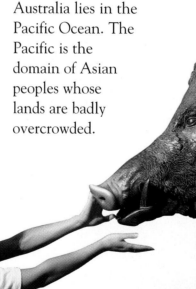

To attract greater numbers of people, Australia welcomed immigrants from all parts of Europe. Previously, most immigrants had come from Great Britain, Ireland, or other selected parts of the old British Empire. Beginning in the late 1940s, newcomers flooded in at the rate of 100,000 a year. They came from Greece, Italy, Poland, and Spain. Some immigrants formed ethnic neighborhoods in Sydney. Signs over stores in Sydney's Newtown and Marrickville neighborhoods changed from English to Greek almost overnight. In the Leichhardt district, more Italian than English was spoken on the streets.

Still, for years after World War II, the government held to what was called a "white Australia" policy regarding immigration. Laws stated that immigrants must come from white European countries. Australia lies in the Pacific Ocean. The Pacific is the domain of Asian peoples whose lands are badly overcrowded.

Many Australians worried that they would be overwhelmed by Asian immigrants if they opened their doors to people from the Pacific. Then, in 1973, the government changed its "white Australia" policy.

By the 1990s, about half the immigrants arriving on Australia's shores were Asians.

Immigrants were called "new Australians." A new Australian was defined as anyone of non-British origins. Today about one-quarter of Sydney's residents are new Australians. People from more than 140 countries live in modern Sydney. The hard-working new Australians help to make Sydney a vibrant international city. Sydney's success story is due largely to the diversity of its people.

A bar of soap with an "I Love Sydney" slogan

By the 1990s, about half the immigrants arriving in Australia were Asians.

Ow yer goin, Mate?

SPEAKING STRINE

Despite Sydney's changing face, some aspects of city life are timeless. Children still go to school dressed in uniforms. The parks are impeccably clean. Sydney Harbor is breathtaking in its beauty. And most of the people speak English—well, sort of.

"Ow yer goin, mate, orright?"

"Yeah, mate. Ow bout you, orright?"

This is a typical exchange between two Sydneysiders, or between a pair of Australians anywhere. It's really not difficult to figure out. Just think of the English language as if the letters *h* and *a* don't exist. Then translate the above exchange as two friends (mates) asking each other, "How's things?"

Left and opposite page right: Waitresses at The Waterfront, a popular restaurant at The Rocks
Below: Australian schoolchildren on a field trip

This special language is an Australian version of English that is loosely called Strine. Language experts say Strine originated in the Cockney English of the lower-class neighborhoods of London in the 1800s. The language was brought to Australia many years ago. Much of Strine is understandable if you simply listen to it for a while. Consider a Sydneysider pricing an item in a store. "Emma chizzit?" he asks. Listen to that a few times. It comes out, "How much is it?" But Strine is much more than just fractured English. Some of Strine's terms are simply amazing.

"Take a squiz," says a Sydney shopkeeper inviting customers through the door. The words mean, "Feel free to look around." Why the phrase "Take a squiz"? Who knows? This is Sydney. Talk as the Sydneysiders talk. For example, shorten a word and add an "o." Thus, Sydney's large suburb of Paddington becomes "Paddo." You may also just shorten a word. That way,

Orright, Mate. Ow bout you?

an annoying mosquito buzzing around your head is a "mozzie." More examples: A politician is a "pollie"; a U-turn, a "U-ie"; lipstick, a "lippie." And someone from Sydney's western suburbs is a "Westie."

A Few Other Strine Terms

Billabong: Waterhole
Chook: Chicken
Make a good fist: Do a good job
Tinny: Can of beer
Tucker: Food
Ute: Pickup truck

THE NEW CITY

Sydney's population has more than doubled since World War II. This dynamic growth has produced a revitalized downtown and an ocean of suburbs. The downtown section lies on the south side of Sydney Harbor. It includes a historic neighborhood called The Rocks and a forest of high-rise office and apartment buildings. Before the war, Sydney's tallest building was only eleven stories high. Today, an eleven-story building is dwarfed by dozens of structures that pierce the city skyline.

The historic Rocks section of Sydney, called the birthplace of the city, has been largely restored and is now a major tourist attraction. This nineteenth-century warehouse is only one of the many restored buildings in the area.

Fifty years ago, much of downtown was made up of buildings constructed in the Victorian style. Victorian buildings featured gingerbread decorations on the outside walls. The Victorian structures made Sydney look like a British town. Many of the old buildings were torn down. In their place rose glass-and-steel towers. Some Australians are not pleased by the new downtown. They say Sydney architects are still imitating others. Sydney once looked like a British town; now it looks like an American city.

Beyond downtown spreads a vast expanse of neighborhoods and suburbs. Sydney is a huge city, covering 670 square miles (1,735 square kilometers). In area, Sydney is three times the size of the American city of Chicago. Yet Chicago and Sydney have roughly the same number of residents. Sydney's sprawl reflects the desire of Sydneysiders to own their own homes. About 70 percent of Sydneysiders are home owners. The suburbs are connected to downtown by a network of highways. Two-car families are common in Sydney.

On hot afternoons, this young Sydney suburbanite enjoys cooling off in her backyard pool.

For the Love of a Bungalow

The prized home for a Sydney family is a three- or four-bedroom bungalow. It is often topped with a red-tiled roof. Most have a small garden, a backyard, and a garage. Sydney has about 1 million of these single-family houses, and they account for the city's sprawl. The city spreads from the harbor area to the hill country many miles inland.

Given their choice, most Sydneysiders would live on the waterfront. However, not everyone can afford a water view, even though water seems to be everywhere in the Sydney area. But many inland home owners have boats in their garages. Access to the sea and a boat dock is just a short drive away for many. Also, families have their own backyard swimming pools or access to public swimming pools. Prosperous Sydney has a way of keeping its residents happy and satisfied.

Scuba divers in Sydney waters use swim fins like these as part of their equipment.

Sydneysiders who can afford it live on the ocean in homes with swimming pools.

Sydney is just a little more than 200 years old. This makes it a young city by the standards of world history. But long before history was written, the people now known as Aborigines caught fish in Sydney's harbor. They also gathered wild berries on shore. The Aborigines came to Australia from Asia more than 40,000 years ago. They crossed over a land bridge that once connected Australia with Asia. The land bridge disappeared, and the Aborigines lived undisturbed on their isolated continent.

THE FIRST FLEET

January 26 is now celebrated as Australia Day. It is the birthday of Australia. It is also Sydney's birthday. Australian history and Sydney's history are intertwined. The modern nation was born on the ground where Sydney stands today. On January 26, 1788, a fleet of eleven ships approached the shores of Australia seeking a good place to start a colony. Commanding the fleet was Captain Arthur Phillip. He sailed into Sydney's natural harbor and wrote, "[I] had the satisfaction of finding the finest harbor in the world."

Today, those eleven ships are called the First Fleet. Battered and leaking, they completed an eight-month voyage from England. The vessels were sent halfway around the globe by the British Home Secretary, Lord Sydney.

European mariners discovered the vast land of Australia. One of those early Europeans was British sea captain and explorer Captain James Cook (above). In 1770, Cook sailed into Botany Bay, near present-day Sydney. Australia's long period of isolation from the rest of the world was about to end.

The painting below shows Cook taking formal possession of the land he named New South Wales.

Aboard the First Fleet's ships were 759 men and women convicts. Thus, Sydney started life with a name and a purpose. The harbor area was called Sydney, after the British Home Secretary. The settlement began as a British convict colony. Previously, the British government had banished law-breakers to its colonies in North America. The American War of Independence brought that practice to an end. Australia now became England's dumping ground for convicts.

Who were these convicts sent to faraway Sydney on the First Fleet? One was Thomas Chaddick. He was convicted of stealing twelve cucumber plants from a private garden. Another was Mary Smith. She stole a pair of leather boots. Other prisoners were punished for being political troublemakers. Some of the convicts had been condemned to death for a variety of offenses. They were spared the hangman or long prison terms by agreeing to banishment in Australia. The huge continent lay 12,000 miles (19,312 km) from England. It was a land the prisoners had probably never heard of before.

The First Fleet, carrying 759 convicts, entered Botany Bay in January 1788.

In addition to prisoners, the First Fleet carried about 250 sailors and guards. Together, the convicts and guards formed a harsh society. Guards were free to punish convicts with up to 500 lashes with a whip. Prisoners were formed into chain gangs. The chain gangs fought guards as well as other prisoners. The alcoholic drink rum became more valuable than silver.

Yet the settlement survived. More ships arrived bringing free men and women who established farms and trading posts.

Captain Arthur Phillip inspects the convict settlers in 1788.

The Australian colony of New South Wales developed with Sydney as its capital. In the years to come, it became fashionable for a Sydney resident to boast that he or she had an ancestor with the First Fleet. It made no difference that the ancestor had probably been a condemned criminal. That long-ago relative was also a genuine Australian pioneer.

The story of the First Fleet had a happy ending. The Aborigines, however, were losers in the nation-making epic. The Aborigines had lived for thousands of years in their own world. They were woefully unprepared for the sudden onslaught of white settlers. The original Australians died in large numbers from European diseases such as smallpox and diphtheria. No pitched wars were fought between Aborigines and whites. Instead, the Aborigines were simply swept aside as whites claimed the land.

After the arrival of the first convict ships, thousands of free settlers came to Sydney. Families established farms and trading posts and the population of Sydney grew.

Captain Bligh

A controversial figure in early Australian history is Captain William Bligh. He served as governor of Australia beginning in 1806. Before becoming governor, Bligh was a harsh sea captain who was overthrown by his angry crew. The rebellion was immortalized in a book and in two movies entitled *Mutiny on the Bounty*. A stern-faced statue of Captain Bligh now stands near Sydney Harbor.

THE CITY AND ITS HARBOR

Sydney Harbor contains more than 21 square miles (54 km²) of deep water. It has about 152 miles (245 km) of shoreline. Hundreds of ships can rest securely in this huge bay. As Australian industry developed, goods made in the country were shipped through the port of Sydney. The great natural harbor was the key to Sydney's growth.

Sydney Cove (now Sydney Harbor) as it looked about about 1803

Sheep and wool products were Australia's first major industry. In 1797, a Sydney settler named John Macarthur brought merino sheep to Australia. Sydney pioneers then discovered passes through the Blue Mountains. The Blue Mountains rise 50 miles (80 km) west of the harbor region. Beyond the mountains lay a virtual ocean of grassland. The endless grasses were perfect grazing country for sheep. By 1850, Australia had only 400,000 people. But some 13 million sheep lived on the land. Wool was processed and shipped abroad through Sydney. The owners of wealthy sheep ranches built luxurious houses in Sydney's downtown area.

Above: Shearing the sheep in Australia in the late 1800s
Below: A sheepskin rug

Next, the lure of gold brought masses of people into Sydney. In 1851, a prospector named Edward Hargraves struck gold in a bleak area about 130 miles (209 km) from Sydney. Hargraves was a Sydney resident. Earlier he had rushed to California, but found no gold there. Then, to his astonishment, he discovered the precious metal on his native Australian soil.

Eventually, the center of the gold industry shifted south to the city of Melbourne. But Sydney Harbor remained the gateway to Australia. Prospectors and goods entered the country through Sydney.

By 1890, the population of Sydney neared 400,000 and had spread along its complex coastline. Citizens rode ferryboats from one part of town to another.

An Australian prospector searches for gold near Sydney after a gold strike in 1851.

Launch parties were popular with early Sydneysiders. This undated photo shows a group of Australians enjoying a day on the water.

The harbor was a great watery traffic jam. Many of the ferryboats were painted green and white. Sydneysiders grew to love them.

Poems and popular songs were written in praise of famous boats. Even today, thousands of Sydneysiders commute to and from work aboard ferryboats.

More than 1 million people lived in Sydney by 1930. It was still a very British town.

Only 3 percent of Sydneysiders came from non-British stock. But war loomed on the horizon. World War II brought profound changes to Sydney.

The Australian flag

The Sydney Town Hall, about 1910

WAR AND AFTERMATH

In the early days of World War II, northern Australia was bombed by Japanese planes. The Australian people lived in fear of attack by enemy troops. On the night of May 31, 1942, three tiny Japanese submarines slipped into Sydney Harbor. The submarines launched torpedoes. The harbor erupted in a hellstorm. Guns from warships turned night into blazing day.

Thunderous gunbursts rattled windows in downtown Sydney. One torpedo narrowly missed the U.S. cruiser *Chicago*, which rested at anchor. Another torpedo blew up a ferryboat, killing nineteen people on board. This brief battle was Sydney's only taste of combat. It left an already troubled people deeply frightened. Would Japanese troops storm ashore near their city?

With the help of the U.S. Navy, the Japanese were kept from invading Australian soil.

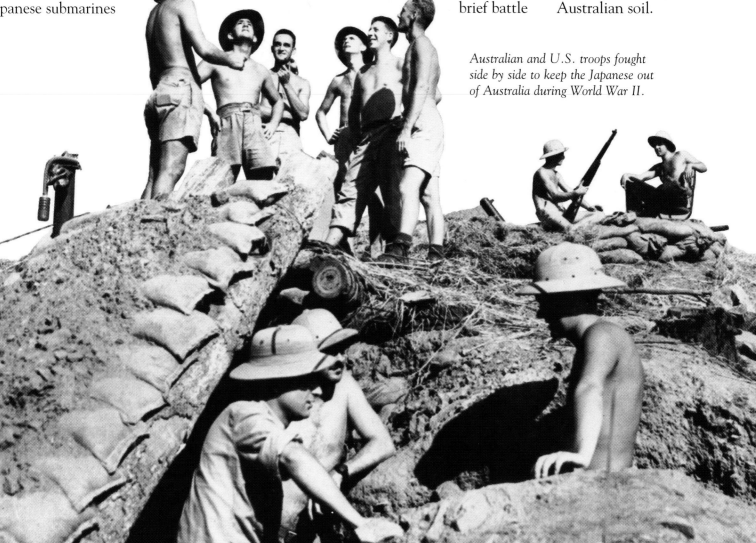

Australian and U.S. troops fought side by side to keep the Japanese out of Australia during World War II.

The war forged a bond of friendship between the United States and Australia. Yanks and Australian troops fought side by side in New Guinea and in other island campaigns. Ships from the two navies pierced deep into enemy-held waters. Affectionately, the Australians began calling the Americans "mates." Americans are still well-liked in the country.

After the war, Australia opened its shores to immigrants. In the next 30 years, more than 4.5 million immigrants came. Australia's population doubled between 1945 and 1975. Sydney benefited from the influx of newcomers. It became the exciting international city we know today.

A torpedo from one of three Japanese midget submarines narrowly missed the U.S. cruiser Chicago (top), which was anchored in Sydney Harbor. Sydneysiders (right) get a closeup view of a crater caused by a shell from one of the submarines.

How prosperous is Australia? Consider these facts: Sydney and other large cities have few slum neighborhoods. Literacy in the nation is nearly 100 percent. The average Australian worker gets four weeks of vacation per year. This vacation policy gives Australians a wealth of leisure time. And Sydney offers many exciting ways to fill leisure hours. The city has superb facilities for pursuing sports and the arts.

Summer in the "Land Down Under"

Australia is called the "Land Down Under" because it lies well below the equator. Being in the Southern Hemisphere means that its seasons are reversed from countries in the Northern Hemisphere such as the United States. The Australian winter lasts from June through August. Christmas and the New Year fall during the hottest time of the year. Pity the poor person in Sydney wearing a Santa Claus suit when the temperature is well into the 90s.

SYDNEY BY THE SEA

It is no wonder that Australians have won many many Olympic medals in swimming and diving. The vast majority of Australian people live near the seacoast. In Sydney's case, the sea is literally everywhere. The Sydney area has 37 public beaches. The beaches are very much a part of young people's summer vacation culture.

Bondi Beach, with its huge expanse of white sand and its ideal waves, attracts sunbathers and surfers during the warm season, from September to May.

Bondi Beach is the city's most popular. All of Sydney was outraged in 1989 when newspapers reported that Bondi's waters were being dangerously polluted by sewer discharges. Sydneysiders demanded that their government clean up the beach no matter what the cost. From September to May (the Australian warm season), Bondi is packed with bathers. Winters are mild in Sydney, but they are chilly enough to discourage swimming. Still, some hardy individuals insist on bathing even in the winter months. Those who swim off the beach in the cold weather are called "Bondi Icebergs."

An American visitor chats with Sydneysiders on Cronulla Beach, the longest beach in the city and the favorite of surfers.

Right: Sydney's lifesavers (lifeguards) show off their precision lifesaving skills during a summer surf carnival.

Below: Swim goggles like these fit snugly against the face and protect a swimmer's eyes from the water.

In Australia, lifeguards are called "lifesavers." Bathers gather to watch them perform a special drill. The lifesavers employ the drill to launch the heavy rowboats they use for rescue purposes. First, five or six stand on either side of a boat. At the leader's command, the guards lift the craft. Marching in precision fashion, the team then heads for the surf. At water's edge, they break into a trot, place the boat on the surface, and climb aboard. On days when towering waves pound the beach, the boat-launching procedure is a tricky business. Yet the lifesavers enjoy their work. Most are unpaid volunteers. Their reward comes from the respect and admiration they receive from bathers.

Surfers are an odd breed. They practice many different forms of their sport. And they are willing to travel the world looking for that perfect wave. Veteran surfers find the ultimate thrill—the exquisite wave—in Sydney. Windsurfers enjoy

A contestant in the Sydney Harbor Yacht Race

skimming the waves on their own surfboard sailboats. Sydney's Long Reef Beach is a magnet for windsurfers. Bodysurfers hold themselves as rigid as statues and let a wave propel them to the beach. The exciting, and sometimes dangerous, sport of bodysurfing is practiced on all Sydney beaches.

Yachting is not for everyone. You have to be rich to own one of the sleek sailing vessels. But anyone can watch the yacht races that begin at Sydney Harbor. The most popular is the Sydney-to-Hobart race, which begins on December 26. Sydney Harbor is a boat jam as thousands of small craft gather to watch the start. Sydneysiders love "messing with boats." A yacht race is a perfect excuse to take to the waters. Wind fills the giant sails when the Hobart race begins. People bobbing about on small boats cheer as the yachts dash out of Sydney Harbor. Hobart lies on the island of Tasmania, 630 miles (1,014 km) away. The yachts will be at sea for more than a week. Gale-force winds will lash the vessels. Still, no crew member would dream of missing this contest. Yachts are the greyhounds of the sea. Let the best craft win!

Windsurfers at Sydney's Long Reef Beach

THE SPORTING LIFE

Sydneysiders are usually a polite, gentle people. They are quick to apologize if they accidentally step on someone's foot. Yet they prefer their football rough-and-tumble. Both professional and amateur versions of Rugby football are played in Sydney. Rugby is not quite as violent as American football. But ferocious tackling and blocking are part of the competition. The familiar game of soccer is preferred by the city's European immigrants. Finally, a bone-crunching game called Australian Rules Football draws wildly enthusiastic fans.

Australian Rugby, though not quite as violent as American football, is one of the world's toughest contact sports.

Australian Rules Football is similar to Rugby. Rules permit players to grasp each other in headlocks. Sometimes an Australian Rules Football game looks like a mass wrestling match. While watching these football contests, Sydney spectators scream, curse, and shout for blood. Then the game ends, and the fans leave the stadium to become polite Sydneysiders once more.

Sydney Football Stadium is packed with avid fans during the Rugby league season.

Another form of Rugby, called Australian Rules Football, is played in Melbourne, capital of the Australian state of Victoria.

Many years ago, the British brought cricket to Australia. It is played now at the Sydney Cricket Ground and on many other fields in the city. Grade schools and high schools sponsor cricket teams. A lively inter-school competition is enjoyed by all. The excitement becomes intense when a British squad visits Sydney. A triumph in cricket is the Australian way of showing the mother country that her son is now a man. Cricket is similar to baseball. Like baseball, it has legendary heroes. One hero is Don Bradman, who played in the 1920s and 1930s. Bradman set records that still stand. He is hailed as the "Babe Ruth" of Australian cricket.

Hundreds of tennis courts stand in Sydney's parks and sports centers. Sydneysiders play tennis with vigor, and they enjoy watching matches as well. The best professional tennis games are held at Sydney's White City Courts. Thousands of spectators crowd into White City to see important contests.

Cricket (above and left), which resembles baseball, is a popular Sydney sport.

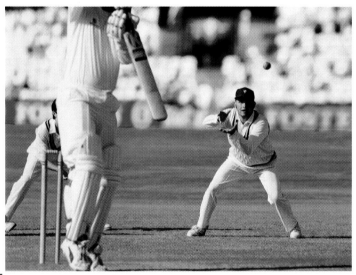

Because no snow falls during Sydney's mild winters, grass skiing has become a popular sport. Students at this summer ski school (left) are using rolling skis on the grass.

Below: Boomerang throwing is an original Australian sport.

Horse racing is also a great spectator sport in Sydney. Naturally, most people go to horse races to place bets. Critics claim Australians have a lust for gambling. It is sometimes said that Australians will bet on two flies climbing up a wall.

Not all sports played in Sydney are imported from Great Britain. Some are Australian originals.

One such sport is boomerang throwing. Yes, Sydney has several fields where people throw boomerangs. What sport could be more Australian? A course near Centennial Park hosts the Boomerang Throwing World Championships. Grass skiing is also practiced in Sydney. And why not?

The city's mild winters prohibit the other kind of skiing. Experienced men and women claim that skiing on wet grass is very similar to skiing on snow. Try it. Just don't break a leg on the slopes.

THE ARTS

The city's busiest center for the performing arts is the Sydney Opera House. More than just opera is presented in this huge building. The opera house also houses a drama theater, a movie theater, a concert hall, and several galleries and restaurants. You need not dress in stiff and formal clothes to enjoy an evening at the opera or theater. Sydneysiders are casual dressers. They prefer to be comfortable during a performance.

Above and left: The Sydney Opera House was designed by architect Jorn Utzon.

Below: An Aboriginal musical instrument called a didjeridu

Sydney has more than 150 art galleries. On most days, the galleries are crowded with browsers and buyers. Local artists claim that Sydney is one of the few cities in the world where a painter or sculptor can actually make a living by creating art. Sydneysiders are proud of their patronage of the fine arts. In Sydney, one can see a sign on the side of a bus advertising a sculpture contest or a showing presented by a new artist.

Left: The Art Gallery of New South Wales

Art of the Original Australians

Aboriginal art is popular in many Sydney galleries. Creating bark paintings and artwork is a cottage industry for many Aboriginal families. Aboriginal craftsmen also produce many fascinating musical instruments. A *didjeridu* is a tubalike instrument made from a hollowed-out tree trunk. A "bullroarer" is a device that is swung above one's head. It produces a deep rumbling sound designed to ward off evil.

"I know the task would be hope-less were I to attempt to make others understand the nature of the beauty of Sydney Harbour. I can say that it is lovely, but I cannot paint its loveliness."

—British writer Anthony Trollope, who visited Sydney in the 1870s

THE HARBOR AREA

Sydney Harbor overwhelms even those who have seen it hundreds of times. Not only is it breathtaking in its beauty, but the harbor is also steeped in Sydney's history. A tiny island in the harbor has the odd name Pinchgut. It is a name out of Australia's prison colony past. Guards once sent disobedient prisoners to Pinchgut, where they were deliberately starved.

The cruise ship Bounty *leaves from The Rocks on a tour of Sydney Harbor.*

Botany Bay

An interesting parkland (one that lies within the city limits) is Botany Bay. It was here, in 1770, that Captain James Cook first stepped ashore. A scientist on Cook's expedition found 3,000 new botanical specimens on the grounds. Therefore, it was named Botany Bay.

Sydney's oldest neighborhood is called The Rocks. It was here that prison laborers built the colony's first huts. The Rocks still contain Sydney's historic buildings. The Rocks was once home to dozens of saloons where drunken sailors got into ferocious fights. Today, quaint old buildings make The Rocks one of the city's major tourist attractions.

Above: The tiny island of Fort Denison was nicknamed Pinchgut in the days when it was used as a place of punishment for convicts.

Right: The Town Crier is one of the tourist attractions at The Rocks.

A stunning landmark is the Sydney Harbor Bridge, opened in 1932. One of the world's great bridges, it is more than 50 football fields in length. Its main feature is the graceful steel arch that seems to leap from one side of the harbor to the other. When it was completed, political leaders called the bridge a "symphony of steel." Today, some Sydneysiders call the bridge the "Coat Hanger" because that's what it resembles. About 200,000 vehicles cross the bridge every day.

A Sydney jacket patch showing the Opera House and the Sydney Harbor Bridge

A view of the Sydney Harbor skyline and the Harbor Bridge at dusk

The best way to see harbor highlights is aboard a tour boat. Most cruise boats leave from a cove called Circular Quay. The name is deceiving. Circular Quay is really rectangular in shape. The boats take tourists into an inlet with the tongue-twisting name Woolloomooloo Bay. The name is Aboriginal, and probably means "young kangaroo." Years ago, kangaroos hopped freely all about the Sydney area.

Tour boats also pass Mrs. Macquarie's Chair, named for the wife of a famous governor. Don't expect to see a chair there. Mrs. Macquarie's Chair is simply a name for an area where people gather to watch boats in the harbor. Some tour boats leave at night and give visitors an elegant Harbor Lights Cruise. No trip to Sydney is complete without a tour of the harbor on board a cruise boat or a ferry.

Above: Most tour boats leave from Circular Quay.

Right: Two young tourists holding stuffed koala bears

CITY ATTRACTIONS

A thrilling view of downtown is offered at the 1,000-foot-(305-m-) high Sydney Tower. Ride the elevator (the lift) to the top. The view from the Observation Deck is decidedly modern. Towering office buildings such as the MLC Center dominate downtown. People often complain that central Sydney is modern to the point of being faceless. But this is not entirely true. Architectural surprises—many of them more than 100 years old—stand in the central city. One such building is the Strand Arcade, built in 1892. Ornate ironwork makes the Strand an architectural gem. Delightful small shops inside the arcade welcome browsers.

Sydney's most popular museums are concentrated in the Darling Harbor neighborhood. The always crowded Powerhouse Museum is built in an old generator station. It holds relics of Australia's past, including the country's first train engines. Hugging

The young men shown below are on a school outing to the Powerhouse Museum (above).

the shoreline is the Sydney Maritime Museum. The museum building is shaped like a giant bursting wave. Outside are craft ranging from small boats to World War II warships. Inside are computer games that challenge you to plot a ship's course from Sydney to Cape Town, South Africa. Also in the Darling Harbor area is the Sydney Aquarium. Unique to this aquarium are fish tanks that run above the heads of viewers. This arrangement allows visitors to gaze up and see menacing sharks peering down at them. A hint: Don't go to see the sharks before you plan to take a dip at one of Sydney's ocean beaches.

Visitors to the Sydney Aquarium are surrounded by fish.

Getting Around in Sydney

Red buses called "Sydney Explorers" transport the bulk of commuters. The city also has a system of trains that run to the distant suburbs. The newest transportation system is a monorail train that connects downtown with Darling Harbor. The swift monorail is an efficient way for tourists to reach Darling Harbor's many museums.

There is no better place to view Australia's strange and wonderful animals than at Sydney's Taronga Park Zoo. Some of the zoo's kangaroos are giants. A male red kangaroo can grow to be 7 feet (2 m) tall and can leap more than 25 feet (7.6 m). Tasmanian devils are also residents at Taronga. The Tasmanian devil is a vicious animal that looks somewhat like a badger. In contrast are the cuddly-looking koalas. They have to qualify as Australia's cutest animals. It is impossible to look at a koala without thinking of a teddy bear. Another Australian native at the zoo is a bird called a kookaburra. Its call sounds like a loud human laugh. An Australian children's song immortalizes the kookaburra and its laugh:

Above: A girl feeding a baby kangaroo

Far right: A koala

Below: a kangaroo magnet

Kookaburra sits in the old gum tree,
Merry merry king of the bush is he!

Laugh, kookaburra! Laugh, kookaburra!
Gay your life must be!

Sydneysiders regard their parks as vital breathing spaces. The parks are kept spotless. Flowers and bushes are carefully tended. Sprawling Centennial Park has bridle paths and duck ponds. The Domain Park is loved for its free music called Under the Stars Concerts. Moore Park hosts a ten-day Royal Easter Show where farmers display prized animals and farm produce. The Royal Botanic Gardens are lush with flowers native to Australia. Bicentennial Park, at the western end of the harbor, lies near the site where the Olympic Games of the year 2000 will be held.

Animal crossing signs in Australia warn of koalas, rather than deer or moose.

Right: The Royal Botanic Gardens as they look in mid-November

EXCITING EXCURSIONS

Hiking for pleasure is called "bushwalking" in Australia. Bushwalking clubs abound in Sydney. Within a 60-mile (97-km) radius of downtown are a fantastic variety of nature preserves. Parks and protected areas make up about 20 percent of the land surrounding the city.

Beloved among the bush areas is Royal National Park. It is located about an hour's drive south of downtown. Established in 1879, it is the second oldest national park in the world. Only Yellowstone in the United States is older. Bushwalkers at Royal National Park take trails carved out centuries ago by Aborigines. The trails cut through forests and past waterfalls. More than 200 types of birds inhabit the park. Visitors listen for the whip bird, whose call sounds like a whip being cracked.

Fifteen miles (24 km) to the north of the city is Ku-ring-gai National Park. Here, more than 57 square miles (148 km^2) of bushland await guests. Aboriginal rock art is a feature of Ku-ring-gai. Ages ago (no one is sure of the dates), Aborigines chiseled scenes of animals and hunters on rock faces. Bushwalkers now hike miles to admire the ancient artworks.

The Three Sisters rock formation in the Blue Mountains at Katoomba

Ku-ring-gai also has an attractive wildflower garden. It is best to visit the garden in September, the Australian spring, when flowers are in glorious bloom.

The Blue Mountains rise to Sydney's west. From a distance, they look blue. The color comes from oil secreted by eucalyptus trees. As the oil evaporates, it leaves a blue haze. Eucalyptus leaves are also the favorite food of the teddy bear-like koalas. Only rarely are koalas seen in the wild here. They are shy creatures and hide from the human beings who tramp about their forest home. Most tourists in the Blue Mountains visit a rock formation called the Three Sisters at Katoomba. According to an Aboriginal legend, a chief once turned his daughters into pillars of stone in order to protect them from evil spirits. Now they stand like three rock soldiers, guarding their father into eternity.

Excursions into the bush end with a return to Sydney. Many Australian vacations conclude with a final trip to Sydney's famed Opera House. It is one of the outstanding buildings in the world. But the Opera House is only one of Sydney's many fascinating sights. Australia's first and largest city continues to charm the many visitors who come each year.

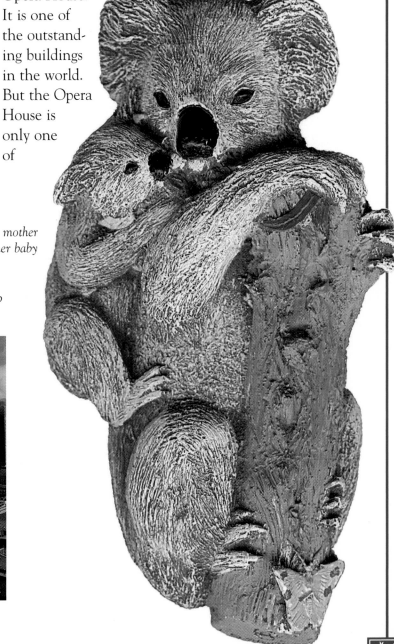

A sculpture of a mother koala with her baby

Many excursions into the bush end with a return to Sydney and a final trip to the Sydney Opera House.

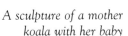

FAMOUS LANDMARKS

The entrance to the Taronga Zoo

Sydney Tower

Right: The Sydney Opera House

Sydney Opera House
Completed in 1973, the Opera house is now the proud symbol of Sydney. Its multiple roofs are built to look like the sails of a ship. Inside are an opera theater, a large concert hall, a drama theater, a movie theater, and a series of galleries and restaurants.

Sydney Harbor Bridge
Some Sydneysiders affectionately call this bridge the "Coat Hanger" because of its gently curved span. When completed in 1932, it eased traffic in the harbor by eliminating the need for ferryboats to carry commuters between downtown and North Sydney.

Circular Quay
Circular Quay (an inlet that is actually rectangular in shape) is the historic heart of Sydney. The members of the First Fleet disembarked here more than 200 years ago. Today, harbor cruise boats carrying tourists leave from this small bay.

Conservatorium
The Conservatorium is a handsome building that was designed as a stable to lodge the governor's horses. It looks like a castle. Now it is a concert hall and music school that presents many free performances.

Taronga Park
A park sitting high on the shore of the harbor, Taronga is famous for its marvelous harbor views and its zoo. The zoo is a wonderful place to see the animals of Australia—including dingos (wild dogs), kangaroos, and shy platypuses.

Hyde Park Barracks
An imposing reminder of Sydney's convict colony past, this building dates to 1819. It was designed by a convict named Francis Greenway and built as a barracks for other convicts. Over the years, it has been used as a lodging place for single women, an orphanage, and a museum.

Mint Museum
Coins were once minted in this building, constructed in the 1840s. Early Australian coins are now displayed in glass-enclosed cases. The building was originally a hospital, one of Sydney's first.

The Conservatorium

Manly Beach

*Sydney Harbor Bridge
and Sydney skyline*

Chinese Gardens
The gardens are a peaceful island in the heart of Darling Harbor. They were designed by landscape experts from Guangzhou, China. Guangzhou is designated as Sydney's sister city. It is a refreshing small park where one can relax among miniature lakes and waterfalls.

Sydney Tower
Sydney's tallest structure, the tower is a needlelike shaft that gives people a dizzying view of the city. Visitors ride elevators on a 41-second ascent that is sure to tickle one's belly. Two restaurants that slowly rotate operate from the Observation Deck. Below is a shopping center called Centrepoint.

Paddington Village Bazaar
More than 250 stalls make this Paddington neighborhood flea market the largest in the city. It is open only on Saturdays. Jugglers, mimes, and other street entertainers come to the market to delight crowds.

Powerhouse Museum
A favorite with children, the museum features many "hands on" exhibits. Children are challenged with computer quizzes and intriguing video games. Themes vary from Australian social history to science and math. The museum occupies a huge old generating station.

University of Sydney
Australia's oldest university operates on this campus. This institution—along with Macquarie University; the University of Western Sydney; the University of Technology, Sydney; and the University of New South Wales—make Sydney an intellectual leader.

Manly Beach
One of the city's prettiest beaches, Manly is usually less crowded than the always popular Bondi Beach. Manly features a boardwalk lined with towering pine trees. It also has an interesting collection of marine life in the Manly Oceanarium.

FAST FACTS

POPULATION   1995   3,770,170

AREA   670 square miles (1,735 km²)

NEIGHBORHOODS Sydney is clustered around its huge harbor. Sydney Harbor (also called Port Jackson), with its many inlets and islands, has more than 152 miles (245 km) of shoreline. Downtown Sydney is located on the south side of the harbor. George Street is a major thoroughfare that runs through the center of downtown. Neighborhoods and suburbs spread out from the harbor region. About 70 percent of Sydney residents own their own homes.

CLIMATE Sydney has a mild climate that allows outdoor activities in both summer and winter. Since Australia lies in the Southern Hemisphere (below the equator), its seasons are the reverse of those in North America or Europe. Summer comes in December, January, and February. Summers can get very hot and humid, and temperatures can reach 100 degrees Fahrenheit (37.7° Celsius). Midwinter comes in July and winter is from June to August. Even during winter, the temperature rarely drops below freezing.

INDUSTRIES Factories in the Sydney area employ about 17 percent of the workforce. Chief products include clothing and processed food. Most factories are in outlying suburbs. Sydney serves as a cattle and wool market for nearby ranches. The harbor makes the city one of the great seaports of the world. Sydney has three commercial television stations and two public broadcasting stations. It also has many government workers, as it is the capital of the Australian state of New South Wales. The city serves as the banking and financial center for the nation.

CHRONOLOGY

40,000 years ago
Aborigines reach Australia; it is believed the Aborigines came from Asia across a land bridge that once connected Australia to the Asian continent

1606
Dutch explorer Willem Jansz visits the Australian coast at present-day Queensland

1770
Captain James Cook sails into Botany Bay and claims the region for Britain

1788
Captain Arthur Phillip and the First Fleet arrive and establish a settlement at Sydney Harbor

1800
John Macarthur begins raising merino sheep in Sydney, thereby starting Australia's first major industry

1813
Explorers penetrate the Blue Mountains beyond Sydney and find excellent pastureland for sheep

1851
A gold strike heralds a gold rush; Sydney's population doubles to almost 100,000 in the next ten years

1879
The Royal National Park is founded south of Sydney

*Young girls playing in
the surf at Manly Beach*

1908
Sydney's population is now
more than half a million

1932
The Sydney Harbor Bridge is
opened

1942
Three Japanese submarines
attack ships in Sydney Harbor
during World War II

1947
The Australian government
opens immigration to non-
British Europeans

1973
The Sydney Opera House is
completed; the Australian government ends its "white
Australia" policy and opens
immigration to people from
Asian nations

1988
Huge parties are held in Sydney
and other cities to celebrate
Australia's 200th birthday

1992
The Sydney Harbor Tunnel
opens to car traffic and reduces
traffic jams on the Sydney
Harbor Bridge

1993
The International Olympic
Committee announces that
Sydney will host the Olympic
Games in the year 2000

SYDNEY

A B C D E F G H I J K

Sydney Harbor Bridge —

Sydney Harbor

Sydney Opera House

Fort Denison

Pinchgut Island

Mrs. Macquarie's Chair

THE ROCKS

Circular Quay

Bennelong Point

Conservatorium

Darling Harbor

Royal Botanic Gardens

Woolcamooloo Bay

MLC Center

Mint Museum

Sydney Maritime Museum

Domain Park

Sydney Aquarium

Hyde Park Barracks

Sydney Tower

Chinese Gardens

White City Courts

CHINATOWN

Powerhouse Museum

University of Sydney

Sydney Cricket Ground

Paddington Village Bazaar

Moore Park

NEWTOWN

Centennial Park

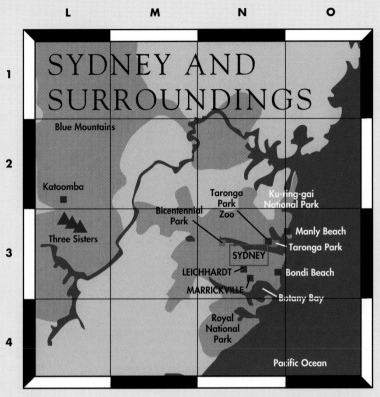

L   M   N   O

SYDNEY AND SURROUNDINGS

Blue Mountains

Katoomba

Three Sisters

Bicentennial Park

Taronga Park Zoo

Ku-ring-gai National Park

Manly Beach

Taronga Park

SYDNEY

LEICHHARDT

Bondi Beach

MARRICKVILLE

Botany Bay

Royal National Park

Pacific Ocean

GLOSSARY

abound: To be great in number, many

bouzouki: Guitarlike stringed instrument popular in Greece

eucalyptus: A tree native to Australia; in Australia it is often called a gum tree

fashionable: Conforming to the latest style in clothing or jewelry

hardy: Strong, full of life

legendary: Famous, the subject of legends

lust: Passionate desire

merino: Breed of sheep, originally from Spain, known for its fine wool

onslaught: Invasion

revere: To love greatly

vibrant: Full of life, highly charged

vitality: High energy

woefully: Pitifully or poorly

Picture Identifications

Cover: Sydney Opera House, girls with koala, kangaroo magnet
Page 1: A boy resting in a waterfront park after a bike ride
Pages 4–5: The Opera House and Sydney Harbor Bridge
Pages 8–9: Sydney schoolgirls
Pages 20–21: Sydney Harbor, 1895
Page 21: An Aboriginal bark painting in the Australia Museum, Sydney
Pages 32–33: Surf-boat racers at a lifesavers' surf carnival, Wonda Beach
Pages 44-45: Sydney Harbor Bridge, Lavender Bay

Photo Credits ©:

INDEX

Page numbers in boldface type indicate illustrations

TO FIND OUT MORE

BOOKS

Browne, Rollo. *A Family in Australia*. Families of the World series. Minneapolis: Lerner Publications, 1987.

Cobb, Vicki. *This Place Is Lonely: The Australian Outback*. New York: Walker and Co., 1994.

Cranshaw, Peter. *Australia*. People and Places series. Parsipanny, N.J.: Silver Burdett, 1988.

Crump, Donald J. *Surprising Lands Down Under*. Washington, D.C.: National Geographic, 1989.

Darian-Smith, Kate and David Lowe. *The Australian Outback*. New York: Thompson, 1995.

Disher, Garry. *The Bamboo Flute* (fiction). New York: Ticknor and Field, 1993.

Kent, Zachary. *Captain James Cook*. The World's Great Explorers series. Chicago: Childrens Press, 1992.

Paterson, A. B. *Waltzing Matilda* (fiction). New York: Harper Collins, 1991.

Place, Marian. *Gold Down Under*. New York: Macmillan, 1969.

ONLINE SITES

Art Gallery of New South Wales
http://www.visitorsguide.aust.com/~tourism/
sydney/attracts/nsw/art/gallery.html
View Aboriginal and other Australian art, as well
as art from Asia, Europe, and North America.

Australian Museum
http://www.austmus.gov.au/
Learn about people, nature, architecture,
Australia, and the earth.

National Parks
http://www.acr.net.au/npws/
Explore the national parks of New South Wales.
Features maps, photos, and links to other parks.

Powerhouse Museum
http://www.phm.gov.au/
Exhibits on science, technology, outer space,
and the everyday lives of Australians.

Sydney
http://www.aust.emb.nw.dc.us:80/map/html/
syd.htm
Tons of information, including the history,
attractions, climate, sports and recreation, and
industry of Sydney.

Sydney Interactive Visitors Guide
http://host.webwin.com/tourism/sydney/
Visit museums and art galleries, study history and
maps, learn about attractions and festivals, and
learn lots more about Sydney, the "jewel of the
South Pacific."

Sydney Olympics
http://www.tourism.nsw.gov.au/aboutNSW/
olympics.html
Learn what New South Wales is doing to prepare
for the 2000 Summer Olympic Games, to be held
in and around Sydney.

Sydney Opera House
http://www.soh.nsw.gov.au/
Learn all about this world-famous opera house —
an entertainment complex under shells!

Welcome to Australia
http://www.aussie.net.au:83/pl/atc
This is the gateway to Australia tourism
information — facts and figures, color photos,
attractions, events, stories from travelers, and
more!

Welcome to Sydney
http://www.slnsw.gov.au/sydney/sydney.htm
Links to some of Sydney's greatest attractions,
including the Museum of Contemporary Art, the
Sydney Opera House, Taronga Zoo, The Rocks
Visitor Center, the National Maritime Museum,
Historic Houses, the Royal Botanic Gardens, and
Darling Harbor.

ABOUT THE AUTHOR

R. Conrad Stein was born and grew up in Chicago. After serving in the Marine Corps, he attended the University of Illinois, where he earned a degree in history. The author now lives in Chicago with his wife and their daughter Janna. Mr. Stein has published more than eighty books for young readers, most of them on history and geography.